The Book

Poems and Pictures

by Corinne Walsh
featuring photographs by LuAnne Underhill

All photographs (including the cover and "About the Author" page) by LuAnne Underhill.
The inside cover page photo and photographs on pages 23 and 49 by Corinne Walsh.

First paperback edition 2021
Second paperback edition 2022

Copyright © 2022 by Corinne Walsh

ISBN 978-1-66782-827-5

for Lu, the best part

. . . What if you slept
and what if
in your sleep
you dreamed
and what if
in your dream
you went to heaven
and there plucked a strange and beautiful flower
and what if
when you woke
you had the flower in your hand
ah, what then ? . . . .
                              -Samuel Taylor Coleridge

Online dating is a dreamscape, and what remains when we wake is often a mystery (or even a new tattoo). During covid I didn't sleep much and dreaming was scarce, until I met Lu online. We made a unique connection through words and photographs. Not actually speaking to each other in person for the first six months, we came to doubt each other's existence in real life. Trusting a stranger, and allowing imagination to become the substance of emotion, made reality painfully mysterious and poetic. We met, finally, in North Carolina after 7 months of correspondence. What remains is the poetry in this chapbook, a chronicle of our journey.

Contents

Infatuation

This morning the sky is a soft pale pink between
the horizon and the clouds — her shoulder is exposed
and there's the full moon, unwilling to let the night go.
As the colors soften like slow music,
and the sunrise dance begins
I listen for the morning song,
my lungs expanding, with the pink orange rays.
As the new day starts to rise,
I am hopeful, content,
and I know what I am
afraid of.

Covid Crush

I keep writing a love poem to a woman
I've never met.
It's a prayer. It's a promise
not to be kept.
The love is not real it's just a dream,
the hope of a life I'll never see.
I keep writing and can't seem to stop,
the worse it gets, the more I want.
She's shut the door and wisely so
and I promised not to knock,
but I can't help it —
I keep on writing and may not stop.
Online love starts like the sweetest song:
a piano playing single notes,
but then the words
keep coming after the tune is done.
I lied and tried to make something out of nothing
and the nothing worked too well, and now
every day I check my profile looking for you,
trying to remember what has never been.
Can you imagine a love more true?

If We Met

If we met,
you would be real
and I would disappear,
softly as the dew
on an autumn morning.

If we met,
you would shine
and I would fade,
like the high clouds
on a summer day.

If we met,
your heart would pound
like a steady drum in the parade,
but mine would knock softly
on the door of your little house
(empty now because you are off
meeting me).

If we met,
only one of us
would be free from regret.

New Terrain (Drift and Drag)

Wheels spinning
on the track
inside my brain.
Racing toward you
fire from within.
Horses
thunder
exhausted from the flames.
Sliding in synchronous
emotion
never touching
the fleeting
shadow of
anticipation.
A mechanical dance
pitting the engines
of high powered
torque and
ignition
against each other.
Speed and precision
locked together
and burning fuel
to make the horses run,
while we hold on
waiting
to stop
at the finish line.

Anticipation

When I wonder
whether anyone will
ever touch me again
I decide to want.

When I think
that my heart is ruined
and love will
never come again,
I decide to know.

How did I come to feel your kindness,
and know your heart when we have never met?
Why do I want you to know me?
How do I know you are what I need?

Once you whispered into the night
and your voice was calm and kind,
carrying words across the sea,
where I was waiting and believed.

38 Days of You

1. Found you by accident
2. You smiled back
3. I Delighted in you
4. Wasn't ready for you (and hid myself)
5. Disappointed you
6. Made you angry
7. Let you alone to think
8. You wanted to understand and forgive
9. Sent you flowers, (but to the wrong address)
10. Adored your kindness
11. Wondered about you
12. Got lost in a fantasy of you
13. Watched you drift away
14. Wrote you a letter (and mailed it to you)
15. Hoped you knew what to do
16. Imagined your world
17. Fought for you in my heart
18. Tattooed you on my hand
19. Found you again online

20. Messaged you
21. Trusted you, (but withheld from you still)
22. You tried to accept me
23. Greedily I devoured your inspiration
24. Listened to you
25. Let you hurt me
26. Told you how I felt
27. You knew what to do
28. Lamented the possible loss of you
29. Could not let you go
30. Accepted your kindness
31. Expressed my gratitude to you
32. Set you free
33. Hid you in my heart
34. Still adore you
35. Remember you
36. Still dream of you
37. Wrote you down
38. Changed by you

LuAnne Knows What To Do

She fixes broken birds,
feeds them blueberries with
her freckled fingers.
Sometimes she hides them
in boxes with lids
until they are healed.
Then she sets them free with
a kind word and her loving touch,
off they fly like it was nothing much.
If something broken needs repair,
or something helpless is in need,
then Lu knows what to do.
No judgement just relief,
her shelter is a gift.
So many birds regain their flight,
return to their wild and precious life.
She listens and often waits for their return,
expelling doubt with her concern.
Never judgement, just relief.
You will find the story
in The Book of Lu.
It's a fledgling tale,
like when a journey finds its own course,
and shows us only souls who can,
(or may learn how to) fly,
deserve to inhabit
the freedom of the sky.

Blind Desire

I want to meet your horses
I want to look into your changing eyes
I want to watch your slender legs walk ahead of me
I want to nuzzle into your neck until you make me stop
I want to see where you have tattoos
I want to smile face to face
I want to find you for the first time in the dark
I want to know how it's possible to feel this way
about a person I have never met.

Fugitive

At any moment I expect you will wake and want
to take your life back from my clenched jaw and aging teeth.
Your wounds won't heal quickly, but you will recover
and sail away — while I stare into the sun hoping to go blind.
I can't unsee you or unfeel you, and when I caught you in my trap
it was for survival not for sport. I couldn't take the pain
but when I fired my shot into the mirror, I hit you instead.
I've been covering my tracks ever since, and now I'm just waiting
to be found out. If I had to do it all again I would do it right,
and I'd be gone already. That could only have been better.
For now, I can only hide in the body of your kindness.

Declivities
(a downward
                slope
        declination
                descent

    Inclination

                cliff
        declining

    descending

        downgrade,
                drop,

        fall).

Why is it called falling in love,
        how is it a descent?

                (Plunge,
                pitch,
        declension?

Is it because the depths of despair,
                and the pains
                        of love
                are too steep

                to overcome?

                Scarp) !

Holding Pattern

When I hold you,
it's with cupped hands,
like I'm holding cool fresh water,
and I don't want to miss a drop.
But when we touch,
I know I never had you,
like a breeze you wander off.
You see me on the outside
while I'm hiding underneath.
You held me only with your gaze.
We may never be as close as one
but I hope this feeling stays.
I'll drink you in, and you'll fly free,
and none will be the wiser.

Fairy Tale

Once there was a woman
(just this one woman one time),
who trembled at the possibility of
the truth speaking its own name.
She wanted to be chosen,
for just a moment to be "the one."
Of all the glittering choices,
she wanted to stand out.
She feared the truth, this woman did,
and for good reason ran and hid.
But then the truth came calling,
as oftentimes truth does.
In her panic, she ran,
but there was no escape from the truth
(poor thing). The faster she ran,
the sooner the truth
caught up to her,
and the further she fled,
the closer it came.
She begged it not to speak its name
but the truth replied,
"I'm not to blame."
The woman wept in shame,
and with no way to escape
nothing stayed the same.

Not Love Poem

Love is
not a flying fish
or a rain cloud overhead.
Love is
not the ocean
and never the sky alone.
Love is
not bitterness
or regretful shame.
When heart sounds cheer,
love is
not jealous or greedy or
afeard.

Love is
the other end of a mysterious
beginning
and the very middle
of good-bye.
Love is
the sigh and the tear.
Love hurts when it heals,
but never turns its back.
Love never shies away.
Love is only grateful when it's done
and then it's not.

End of the Story

You won't light the match
To burn this bridge
and I won't cross it
to let you see my face.
Stay busy in your yard
and I'll keep writing
postcards I'll never send.
Love is not wasted
if it stays planted in the ground.
You're free and so am I
Caterpillar, Chrysalis, Butterfly!
The only danger I've come
to fear is your good-bye.
I feel the end but I can't let go
like a kite string all run through,
you're sailing away from me
out of reach
to the end of the story.

Hope

This grasping thing.
This monster growing from inside,
ignores what I want or need.
It's feeding on your oxygen, and your appetites.
I stay busy, doing chores to distract myself from the apprehension
and sudden, unstoppable feeling,
insatiable and bigger than I am, getting stronger each day
consuming me in large bites, how will it end?
When will it be over?

Not today, not while I'm chasing it around in the sand barefoot.

Undignified infatuation is laughing at me — it's loving me,
taunting me with soft kisses, heating up my skin from the inside,
and I can only wait and want (want more than wait).
Til I want all there is,
greedy, gaudy, gaping like a wound refusing to heal,
I'm lost within the blasting echo of its sound.
While you sit there calmly watching me, wanting you
as if my wanting feeds your monster,
and all I can do is bring up the recycling bins
and mow the lawn.

Upstairs in the Triangle of Wood and Whimsy
(at your A-Frame house on the golf course in North Carolina)

I'm writing this little poem in the dark.
You are up in the kitchen, downstairs
and I don't want to interrupt your morning dance.
The creaking of the floorboards under your socked feet,
the sliding of drawers and cupboards, and the soft sound
of a teaspoon spooning sugar are measuring your movements
like the music of memory.
The warming smell of coffee is mingling
with the soft breaths of the early day, now wandering
in with bird sounds through the open sliding glass door.
You are mostly quiet except for your half whispering
morning graces to the cats and dog.
I'm levitating upstairs among the cross beams,
scribbling away,
in the last moments of night's shadows and solitude,
grateful for the soft bed you made me up here.
Resting in peaceful comfort, I'm not sure if I'm not dreaming
as I listen to you open your world to the new day,
and offer it to me in the melting darkness.

Reflection on the Grass

Things we've never spoken about,
the things we've never said
are all the things I think about
and have trapped inside my head.
You got me hooked on beauty,
I now know where it lives.
Plump pine trees line the fairway
and stand tall in your backyard.
The rising sun comes creeping,
its beauty cannot be undone.
We have become connected
just by looking in the same direction,
and knowing when a moment lasts.
You have taught me how to see
the reflection on the grass.
These things we've never spoken of
will be the things that last.

Let's Stay Strangers, Lu!

When I tried to make eye contact with you
for the first time, I was too afraid.
Scared of what I might see
in your eyes reflected back, I hesitated.
Then the moment passed,
and then I couldn't stop looking at you.
Everything about you true and
real, beautifully "exceeding expectations."
Has the moment passed, again?
Let's always have secrets that we keep
from each other, Lu.
Tell me only what should be revealed
to a stranger.

When I am a Poet

I'm a poet when I swim:
I made this poem in the pool,
reaching out and pulling in.
Words are like water when you swim.

I'm a poet when I'm doing laundry:
loading, soaking, spinning –
the running water washes loose the words.
I collect them from the lint trap in the end.

I'm a poet when I give my kids a bath:
whole stanzas can arrive in just a splash,
and as the bubbles exit down the drain,
I smile when the foolish rhymes remain.

I'm a poet when I'm sailing:
flying on the glassy sea,
drifting, rocking in my little boat,
swallowing the words rising in my throat.

I'm a poet when I dream:
setting words free in a stream
watching them disappear as I let them go,
sinking into the mud below.

I'm not the poet of my dreams.
My poems get lost in the morning when I wake.
When I put my feet upon the floor,
I rise and find I'm nothing more
than the person in the dark before.
Then all the tiny pieces fall away,
only what other people see, and need can stay.
All the happy singing words go free.
They fly off to find another poet who is not me.

At Last

Finally, You sitting across from me
while I worry about the light —
you can see every whisker,
and every line of uncertainty
but you smile anyway,
and I love you just for that.
You cut the kiwi slices perfectly.
You know just what to do!
Your orange Wheaties bowl,
a collectible treasure trove, is so you.
Mostly we laugh.
We don't stop even when it hurts.
I knew in the first five minutes
it was the time for us.
Maybe you wanted the same thing,
for just a solid moment
you ached for it like me.
Being in that moment with you
was worth the crazy quest,
knowing we shared that tiny truth
is a story all its own, like the sky
and how it changes with the clouds,
we can only live beneath its glory and
bask in its sun rays,
until the light dies down
and darkness sets us free.

Sea Glass

I tumbled open
like a box of hidden treasure
hauled up
from the bottom of the sea
after a storm.
You gathered me up,
collecting all the pieces
in your strong slender hands.
Close to ruin,
unrecognizable,
you dusted me off,
cleaned me up,
made me feel beautiful
and sold me off.

A Memory

Do you remember lying
on our backs
together under the fading light
of a Friday afternoon in November?
We were on the dock near your house
at the end of the walking trail.
Your dog died the day before
and you were looking
for the answer in the sky,
both of us searching the clouds
for acceptance and relief.
I remember,
I wanted to stay with you forever.
The thick damp wood of the dock
so stiff under our backs,
not uncomfortable but just
what we needed to keep from
moving closer.
Your voice was making peace
with your pain,
and the clouds were merging
and fading with no other purpose
than to distract you.
There was no time, and no escape
in that tiny inevitable moment
shadowing your sadness
solemnly under the tall pine trees.
Do you remember?

Pardon

You are a poem
to me
not a person
who will let me down
as you change
with the seasons
dropping your leaves
like a tree
and then becoming
a bird in that very same tree
making a beautiful
nest with your leaves
until you fly free
and I watch you float
and soar
(until you have flown away)
no rejection do I feel
because you are a poem
not the woman
I love.

Dreamscape

We touched before we spoke.
In the darkness before first light,
her left hand matching my right
on the screen door between us,
the silvery moon reflecting in her eyes.
More moments passed in silence.
"I won't come in if you don't
want," her whisper broke
the silence.
Releasing the latch on the screen door
it came unstuck.
Our hands still touching,
"Please," she whispered.
Pushing the door open
we met for the first time
in the darkness on the porch.

We sat on the top step,
her head found my shoulder
and rested there in the moonlight.
We sat together
waiting as the distance, in
counted miles softly faded.
The echo of a dog barking
soothed the silence.
More minutes passed,
then her head lifted
from my shoulder
and I turned to meet her eyes.
When she whispered my name,
I kissed her cheek
and ear and eye
then her forehead and other cheek
until I found her lips
waiting for mine
while the waning moon
promised to keep our secret.

On Waking up Alone

Our dreams hold
us fast to sleep,
and waking in real life
opens the daily illusion
that we are any
small part of the world.
Soon enough
each of us is torn
and tattered by
the sharpened teeth
of loneliness
and the bitter taste
of waking up alone.
Knowing that
the person we love
wants nothing
from us lingers at dawn
and drives the day
into a ditch.

If (K)not for Love

If not for love,
we wouldn't make mistakes,
take no wrong turns,
commit no crimes of omission,
sing in perfect pitch and harmony.
If not for love,
we could see clearly
and follow any path.
Justice would prevail.
But love ties us up in knots,
and breaks us down
in the dark.
Dreaming about love, we can't help
being tempted by its promise.
Greedily we swing and miss.
We jump and fall,
and when we lose
"mistake" we call.
Yet failure stops us not.
We crawl, and brawl
and want it all at any price.
If not for love,
loneliness would have no name,
and a broken heart would have no pain.
Flowers would grow but never bloom,
and I would not have met you,
if not for love.

Acknowledgements

So grateful for the collaboration and the added visual perspective provided by LuAnne Underhill's amazing photographs. Her generosity in sharing them only enhances the journey chronicled in *The Book of Lu*. I fell in love with her view of North Carolina, and I hope readers can also appreciate the transformative landscape we have shared. This is the first time in print for Lu Underhill. Her love of nature and animals is undeniable, and her ability to capture and share beauty is a gift. The poems in *The Book of Lu* were inspired in part by LuAnne's unique perspective, and the connection that developed between poet and photographer exchanging words and pictures during the isolation of the Covid pandemic.

Thank you to *The RavensPerch* for previously publishing "38 Days of You," "Anticipation," "If We Met," and "Infatuation."

A heartfelt thank you to Sophia for her patience and expertise in edting and help with the layout design of this chapbook.

P.S. Thank you Duncan and Jakie May for all the comfort, purring, and cuteness.

About the Author

As a small child she wrote little notes and hid them where people might accidently find them, in mailboxes, in pockets, even under rocks. In this, her first chapbook, Corinne Walsh claims her identity as a poet. Composing thoughts and writing down feelings to cast them out into the world started as a child's experiment in expression, now, 50+ years later the habit continues. And, while it's no secret who the intended recipient is here, these poems represent a recent journey of self relection through the course of finding love and friendship in middle age. Enjoy the ride.

About the Photographer

LuAnne Underhill is a lifelong resident of North Carolina. She is also an accomplished self-taught photographer whose love of animals, nature, and music is as much a part of her photography as her eye for beauty. The photographs in this collection represent LuAnne's gift for capturing a moment of change in a familiar landscape. LuAnne is currently semi-retired and awaiting her next adventure.

True North Carolina